1993

To

Ewald

From

Carol

Love Is
Like a Crayon
Because It Comes
in All Colors

Love Is Like a Crayon Because It Comes in All Colors

Children on Love

David Heller

Villard Books New York 1993

Villard Books is a registered trademark of Random House, Inc.

Library of Congress Cataloging-in-Publication Data
Heller, David.
Love is like a crayon because it comes in all colors : children on
love / David Heller.
p.   cm.
ISBN 0-679-41756-7
1. Love—United States—Public opinion.
2. Children—United States—Attitudes.
3. Public opinion—United States. I. Title.
BF575.L8H378   1992
152.4′1—dc20   92-20730

Manufactured in the United States of America

9 8 7 6 5 4 3 2

First edition

*Dedicated with love to all
of the children*

Introduction

To focus on love is to talk about life. Love is essential to our makeup as lovers, as friends, as parents, as children, and as human beings.

While love can be a very serious matter, the act of loving and its participants do have their humorous and lighter sides. Love can be funny too as it reveals so much about the human drama that we all take part in. In fact, the capacity to appreciate the humor in love may well be the first step in gaining an understanding of it.

Who better to capture the dual nature of love than children, who are at once bemused and fascinated by it? Children know firsthand about the love that exists between a parent and child, but they're also surprisingly savvy about the type of love that lies just beyond the horizon for them—intimate love between two people. The youngsters' observations will entertain you, and they will also cause you to ponder how you think about love and how you express it in your own life.

From my ongoing interviews with children, I've collected some of their wisest and funniest morsels about love. I hope that you thoroughly enjoy this compilation and feel moved to share them with a lover or friend. Love is certainly something to share, and the children remind us how rich and heart-warming love is—"the true means by which the world is enjoyed" (Thomas Traherne).

—DAVID HELLER, PH.D.

Love Is
Like a Crayon
Because It Comes
in All Colors

Concerning the Origins of Love

"Cupid kissed God and that got the ball rollin'."
Julio, age 9

"One of the Greek lady gods got a crush on one of
the Greek man gods. He tried to hit her with
lightning and thunderbolts, but he just couldn't get
her away from him. . . . After a while, they became
the first married gods."
Robbie, age 8

"When God saw Miami Beach, He fell in love with
it. . . . That was the first example of love
that is on the record."
Arnold, age 10

"Cavemen started it because they wanted to find out
how to get babies. Before they knew about love,
they thought you could make babies by
swallowing rocks."
John, age 9

"It's probably wonderful to fall in love. It's like you see
rainbows all the time."
Shari, age 9

Concerning Why Love Happens Between Two Particular People

"One of the people has freckles and so he finds
somebody else who has freckles too."
Andrew, age 6

"No one is sure why it happens, but I heard that it
has something to do with how you smell. . . . That's
why perfume and deodorant are so popular."
Mae, age 9

"I think you're supposed to get shot with an arrow
or something, but the rest of it isn't supposed
to be so painful."

Manuel, age 8

On What Falling in Love Is Like

"Like an avalanche where you have to run
for your life."
John, age 9

"If falling in love is anything like learning how to
spell, I don't want to do it. It takes too long."
Glenn, age 7

"If you have a lot of worries, you should make sure you fall in love. . . . All worries will go away."

Jenny, age 8

On the Role of Beauty and Handsomeness in Love

"If you want to be loved by somebody who isn't
already in your family, it doesn't hurt
to be beautiful."

Anita C., age 8

"It isn't always just how you look. Look at me.
I'm handsome like anything and I haven't got
anybody to marry me yet."

Brian, age 7

"Beauty is skin deep. But how rich you are
can last a long time."

Christine, age 9

"I don't think you actually fall in love. I think it's supposed
to be more like diving in."
Janet, age 10

Reflections on the Nature of Love

"Love makes all things grow."
Marie, age 7

"Love is the most important thing in the world, but
baseball is pretty good too."
Greg, age 8

"Love is like a crayon because it comes in all colors."

Janet, age 10

How Do People in Love Typically Behave?

"Mooshy . . . like puppy dogs . . . except puppy dogs don't wag their tails nearly as much."
Arnold, age 10

"Some people act like happy children. So I would say that it's a pretty good thing."
Lynn, age 8

"Love is like a flower. . . . Don't step on it!"
Marv, age 8

"When a person gets kissed for the first time,
they fall down and they don't get up for
at least an hour."
Wendy, age 8

"All of a sudden, the people get movies fever so
they can sit together in the dark."
Sherm, age 8

Concerning Why Lovers
Often Hold Hands

"They want to make sure their rings don't fall off
because they paid good money for them."
Gavin, age 8

"In cold weather, it keeps you both from being
blown away by the wind."
Michelle, age 7

"They are just practicing for when they might have to walk down the aisle someday and do the holy matchimony thing."

John, age 9

"Holding hands is usually a sign that people like each other a lot. . . . Of course, it could mean that they are afraid that somebody else might flirt with their lover."

Christine, age 9

"The main reason that I've seen for why they hold hands is that their parents make them do it."

Douglas, age 5

"Holding hands is a way of saying that you are partners and you are kind of glued together."

Sarah, age 9

Confidential Opinions
About Love

"I am in favor of love as long as it doesn't happen
when *Dinosaurs* is on television."

Jill, age 6

"Love is foolish . . . but I still might try it sometime."

Floyd, age 9

"Yesterday I kissed a girl in a private place. . . .
We were behind a tree."
Carey, age 7

"Nobody can survive without love. It's like air and water. There's no use trying to fight Mother Nature."

Shari, age 9

"Love will find you, even if you are trying to hide from it. I been trying to hide from it since I was five, but the girls keep finding me."

Dave, age 8

"Love is too sloppy . . . especially when there's some other person involved."

Arnold, age 10

"I'm not rushing into being in love. I'm finding fourth grade hard enough."

Regina, age 10

The Personal Qualities You Need
to Have in Order to Be
a Good Lover

"Sensitivity don't hurt."
Robbie, age 8

"One of you should know how to write a check.
Because, even if you have tons of love, there is still
going to be a lot of bills."
Ava, age 8

"The whole world needs love. But it takes some people a lot longer to get around to understanding that."
Sharon, age 9

Some Surefire Ways to Make a Person Fall in Love with You

"Tell them that you own a whole bunch
of candy stores."
Del, age 6

"Shake your hips and hope for the best."
Camille, age 9

"Help them cross the street if they are still little."
Roger, age 6

"Yell out that you love them at the top of your lungs
. . . and don't worry if their parents are right there."
Manuel, age 8

"Just act friendly and smile a lot and they will have
to like you, because you will probably stand out
from most of the other people they know."
Diana, age 8

"Don't do things like have smelly, green sneakers.
You might get attention, but attention ain't the same
thing as love."
Alonzo, age 9

"One way is to take the girl out to eat. Make sure it's something she likes to eat. French fries usually works for me."

Bart, age 9

"If you want someone to love you, be kind and generous and the rest of the stuff that is supposed to happen will take care of itself."

Arnold, age 10

How Can You Tell If Two Adults Eating Dinner at a Restaurant Are in Love?

"Just see if the man picks up the check. That's how you can tell if he's in love."

Bobby J., age 9

"Lovers will just be staring at each other and their food will get cold. . . . Other people care more about the food."

Bart, age 9

"Sometimes a bottle of wine is the dead giveaway."
Arnold, age 10

"Romantic adults usually are all dressed up, so if they are just wearing jeans it might mean they used to go out or they just broke up."
Sarah, age 9

"The people are in love if they don't seem like they're in a hurry for the waiter to come over. Plus they might even leave him a big tip because they are in a real lovers' mood."
Floyd, age 9

"See if the man has lipstick on his face."
Sandra, age 7

"It's love if they order one of those desserts that are on fire. They like to order those because it's just like how their hearts are—on fire."

Christine, age 9

Titles of the Love Ballads You Can Sing to Your Beloved

" 'How Do I Love Thee When You're Always
Picking Your Nose?' "
Arnold, age 10

" 'You Are My Darling Even Though You Also
Know My Sister.' "
Larry, age 8

" 'I Love Hamburgers, I Like You!' "
Eddie, age 6

" 'I Am in Love with You Most of the Time, but Don't Bother Me When I'm with My Friends.' "
Bob, age 9

" 'Hey, Baby, I Don't like Girls but I'm Willing to Forget You Are One!' "
Will, age 7

" 'Honey, I Got Your Curly Hair and Your Nintendo on My Mind.' "
Sharon, age 9

" 'Let's Try Out This Love Thing Even Though
It Sounds Dumb.' "
Dick, age 7

" 'Love Is Good and So Are
Chocolate-Covered Peanuts.' "
Pamela, age 8

"As soon as you say 'I love you' it gets marked down in
heaven and they check up on you to make sure you
are behaving yourself."
Julio, age 9

What Most People Are Thinking When They Say "I Love You"

"They're thinking: I sure love Mary. I hope Mary loves me too. Because if she don't love me, I'm going to have the world's biggest heartache and a giant headache to go with it."
Kenneth, age 10

"Oh my gosh, I'm in love. . . . What will my mother say?"
Sharon, age 9

"The person is thinking: Yeah, I really do love him.
But I hope he showers at least once a day."
Michelle, age 7

"Oh boy, now I've let the cat out of the bag. Maybe
I should of played hard to get?"
Janet, age 10

"People who say 'I love you' are too silly to be
thinking anything at all."
Gerard, age 6

"Some lovers might be real nervous, so they are glad that they finally got it out and said it and now they can go eat."

Dick, age 7

How Was Kissing Invented?

"It went like this. The first people had a big argument and they started wrestling, and then they kind of bumped into each other . . . in the face. . . . That's how kissing started."

Jeremy, age 8

"Kissing was invented as a way to get things going—
otherwise the men would never agree
to get married."
Anita, age 9

"Kissing was invented by a fool, if you ask me, but
he sure has a lot of followers."
Dennis, age 9

"It might have started with the movie *Gone With
the Wind*."
Pam, age 7

"I know one reason that kissing was created.
It makes you feel warm all over, and
they didn't always have electric heat or fireplaces
or even stoves in their houses."
Gina, age 8

How a Person Learns
How to Kiss

"You can have a big rehearsal with your Barbie
and Ken dolls."
Julia, age 7

"You learn it right on the spot when gooshy feelings
get the best of you."
Brian, age 7

"It might help to watch soap operas all day."
Carin, age 9

"If you're nice to her, your older sister might show
you the ropes."
Diana, age 8

"You can learn about it from the gym teacher. He's
always talking about life stuff like that."
Arnold, age 10

When Is It Okay to Kiss Someone?

"When they're rich."
Pam, age 7

"It's never okay to kiss a boy. They always slobber all over you. . . . That's why I stopped doing it."
Tammy, age 10

"One way to learn how to kiss is to watch your mom and dad doing it, but don't let them know you are watching, or else they'll get mad at you."
Corinne, age 6

"You have to be married to kiss somebody on the lips . . . otherwise you're stuck with their cheeks."
Lucy, age 8

"If it's your mother, you can kiss her anytime. But if it's a new person, you have to ask permission."
Roger, age 6

"I look at kissing like this: Kissing is fine if you like it, but it's a free country and nobody should be forced to do it."
Maury, age 7

The Real Story About Romeo and Juliet

"I heard he had another lover, but then it got covered up and you don't hear much about it."
Sandra, age 7

"One of them was like a prince or something and the other was an ugly, ugly princess."
Gino, age 7

"They were just two dumb teenagers who caused a
lot of problems for their parents."
Floyd, age 9

"I think Juliet is my cousin, but I'm not sure."
Bill, age 6

"At the end, they got married but they didn't live
happily ever after. . . . Juliet called Romeo sloppy for
eating with his hands."
Arnold, age 10

Concerning How to Tell
if Love Is Real

"Love is real if you and the other person stick
together like peanut butter and jelly."
Janet, age 10

"Love is either real or it's barforoni. . . .
There's no in between."
Robbie, age 8

"Love is only fake when it's on television. The rest of the time it's for real or else people are trying hard to make it real."

Linda, age 9

"You know it's real when you been married for thirty-seven and a half years. . . . That's the test."

Dave, age 8

How to Make Love Endure

"Spend most of your time loving instead of
going to work."

Dick, age 7

"Don't forget your wife's name. . . . That will
mess up the love."

Erin, age 8

"If you want love to last, save some of it for a rainy day."
Tim, age 10

"Be a good kisser. It might make your wife forget that you never take out the trash."

Dave, age 8

"Don't throw your lover's sports cards on the floor when he's got them all set up for a big trade."

Walker, age 8

"Don't say you love somebody and then change your mind. . . . Love isn't like picking what movie you want to watch."

Natalie, age 9

What Do All Valentine's Cards Have in Common?

"Many of them have $1.50 printed on the back."
Stephanie, age 8

"Most of them have the word 'I' in them,
but that's okay because they also have the word
'love' in them too."
Brett, age 9

"The ones that are sent by ladies have lipstick on them, because that's where they kissed them."
Harold, age 8

"Eventually, they all get around to talking about hugging."
Madolyn, age 8

"Most of the Valentine's cards talk about love and romance and kissing, but then some of them are just friendly so you don't have to be totally embarrassed to be sending them."
Robbie, age 8

The Essential Purpose of Valentine's Day

"To increase the love in the world by
about twenty times."
Michelle, age 7

"To convince wives that the husbands really do love
them, even if the husbands don't say it so good."
Arnold, age 10

"It's a good day to celebrate red if that's your favorite color."
Val, age 6

"You get a last chance to be sweet on that day."
Walker, age 8

"The purpose of Valentine's Day is to show love and
eat chocolates. Believe it or not, I like the love part
as much as the chocolate part."
Carey, age 7

"Love Means Never . . ."

"Love means never calling your husband 'Tubs.' "
Melinda, age 10

"Love means never holding on to your money,
because your wife will be busy spending it."
Floyd, age 9

"Love means never hating somebody just because
they're different on the outside."
Walker, age 8

"If it means you never have time to go fishing,
then love ain't for me."
Danny, age 6

"Love means never saying no. . . . You can
just say: 'Later, dear.' "
Melinda, age 10

"You can never have too much love. We should keep
making it as fast as we can."
Jimmy, age 7

Is There as Much Love Around as There Used to Be?

"We got more love now. . . . And it all comes to a head on Valentine's Day."
Shari, age 9

"I don't think people talk about love as much, but that doesn't mean they don't have it in their hearts."
Melinda, age 10

"It's hard to measure how much love is around. But I've seen a lot of kissin' lately in my family, so I guess it's still pretty popular."

Robbie, age 8

"It's probably always the same amount of love, because God wouldn't play favorites when it comes to love."

Julianne, age 8

"Love is nice. . . . So people will always pick it when they need to find something to do."

Brian, age 7

Concerning What You Can Expect to Find at a Place Called Lovers' Lane

"Plenty of young people with tired lips."
John, age 9

"There's a sign that says: You can't pass through on this road unless you are in love with somebody."
Alicia, age 6

"I bet they sell popsicles there. Lovers always
need to cool off."
Marv, age 8

"I would never go near that lane. . . .
It's too dangerous."
Gerard, age 6

"I bet that lane has a lot of nice curves on it."
Arnold, age 10

Is Love the Same All Over the World?

"Pretty much. But I don't know if everybody kisses. Some wild tribes might rub their backsides together or something like that."

Sean, age 9

"Men and women have fights and then kiss and make up all over the world."

Dave, age 8

ABOUT THE AUTHOR

David Heller is widely known for his popular books about how children perceive the world and experience spirituality. He graduated from Harvard University and holds a Ph.D. in psychology from the University of Michigan. His work has appeared on ABC's *20/20* and in *People, Good Housekeeping, Psychology Today,* and *USA Today.*